WHEN WE WALKED ON THE MOON

WHEN WE WALKED ON THE MOON

DAVID LONG

SAM KALDA

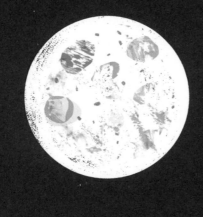

WIDE EYED EDITIONS

CONTENTS

IN MEMORY OF PEENEMÜNDE'S
MANY VICTIMS

GETTING *to the* MOON

"ONE OF THE GREAT ADVENTURES OF OUR TIME"

More than 5,000 rockets have been blasted into space, but only twelve people have ever been lucky enough to walk on the moon and look up at Earth.

Getting them to the moon and back was the single most expensive project the world had ever seen, and a tremendous feat of human engineering. More than 400,000 men and women worked to make the trips to the moon, named the Apollo missions, successful.

Before the Apollo missions, small rockets had already managed to travel into space, starting with the V2 in Germany in 1944. In 1961, the Soviet pilot Yuri Gagarin had become the first man to orbit the Earth. Another rocket had successfully orbited the moon, but no one had yet tried to land on the surface. In what people called the space race, American and Soviet teams were competing to be the first to achieve this.

But to land a human on the moon—and to bring them home safely—required a different kind of rocket, bigger and more powerful than before and massively more expensive.

"IN 1961, THE SOVIET PILOT YURI GAGARIN HAD BECOME THE FIRST MAN TO ORBIT THE EARTH"

This new rocket was called the Saturn V. Like other rockets, it needed to escape Earth's gravity, and then it would need to fly hundreds of thousands of miles through space. And because space is such a hostile, dangerous environment, it had to contain all the technology needed to survive out there, so far from home.

But the Saturn V was also designed to fly faster and farther than ever before. Each one had around three million parts and they are still the largest and heaviest rockets ever launched. An incredible 363 feet from nose to tail, and weighing 3,100 tons, a Saturn V is taller than the Statue of Liberty or Big Ben.

"EACH ROCKET HAD TO CARRY ENOUGH FUEL TO FLY 238,500 MILES"

Each rocket had to carry three astronauts and enough fuel to fly the 238,500 miles to the moon, and all the way back. It would also carry the equipment needed

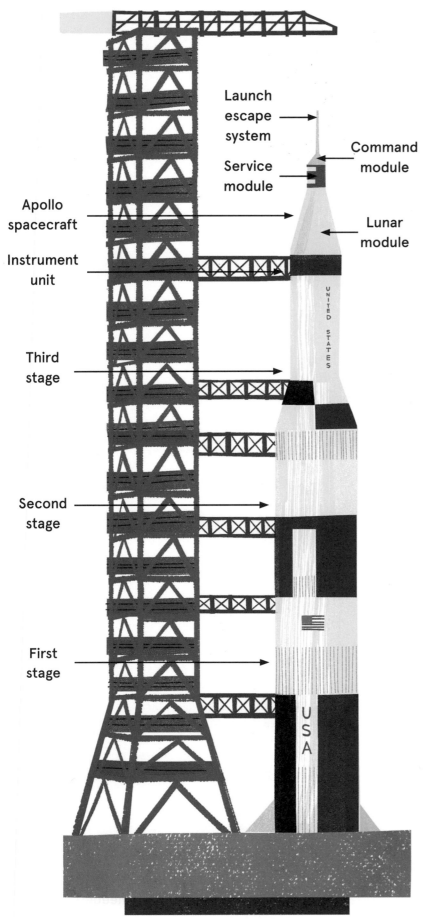

Launch escape system

Command module

Service module

Apollo spacecraft

Lunar module

Instrument unit

Third stage

Second stage

First stage

UNITED STATES

USA

to land on the moon's surface and take off again.

Although the Saturn V was enormous, most of it was taken up by fuel and eleven gigantic engines. A dangerous combination of more than 900,000 gallons of explosive kerosene, liquid hydrogen, and liquid oxygen was needed to launch the rocket beyond the pull of Earth's gravity. It had three modules that the astronauts would use while in space. They would stay in the nose-cone command module during launch. The service module housed the main engine, which would power the craft through space and also provide life-support systems and power for the crew. The lunar module was the part that would travel to the moon's surface.

The first few Saturn V rockets were used in tests to demonstrate that the technology worked safely. Finally, three years after the Saturn V was first created, it was considered safe enough for the first manned mission to the moon. The date was set: July 16, 1969.

WE HAVE LIFTOFF

"THE ENGINES BEGAN THEIR THUNDEROUS ROAR"

Humans had been gazing up at the moon for thousands of years, so the idea that somebody might actually fly to it and be able to gaze back at the Earth was incredibly exciting. On the morning of July 16, 1969, millions of people around the world turned on their televisions to see Neil Armstrong, Buzz Aldrin, and Michael Collins—the crew of Apollo 11—climbing into the capsule.

Hundreds of thousands more, from dozens of different countries, crowded onto boats and beaches surrounding the launch site in Florida. There was a risk the rocket might explode on takeoff, so many spectators were seated more than three miles away, but the sound was still deafening. Buildings trembled and the ground shook as the first five engines ignited and began their thunderous roar. The first journey to the moon had begun.

Inside the capsule, the noise was terrifying, and the whole rocket shook violently as it left the launch pad. Later, out in space, the men would experience the sense of being weightless, but now, as the huge engines powered their machine into the sky, huge g-forces made it almost impossible for the astronauts to move their arms or legs.

"HUGE G-FORCES MADE IT ALMOST IMPOSSIBLE FOR THE MEN TO MOVE THEIR ARMS OR LEGS"

Twelve minutes after launch, the crew of Apollo 11 were traveling at more than 20,000 miles per hour. Even at this speed, it would take almost four days to reach the moon. Seen through the capsule windows, the Earth began to grow smaller and smaller. It was still possible to communicate with Mission Control back home, but radio messages now took several seconds to travel through space. Soon our whole planet looked no larger than a glass marble, an extraordinary sight that no one had ever seen before.

After the first few minutes, the first two stages of the Saturn V had

"IT WOULD TAKE ALMOST FOUR DAYS TO REACH THE MOON, NEARLY 240,000 MILES AWAY"

been discarded. The third stage was jettisoned a few hours later. For the rest of their long, lonely voyage—hundreds of thousands of miles to the moon and back—the three astronauts would be crowded together, eating, sleeping, and floating around inside a tiny capsule.

The capsule was called the command module. Just ten feet high and twelve feet wide, it was dark and cramped with five small windows made of thick glass. It was the only part of the huge rocket that was designed to come back to Earth.

"THE THREE ASTRONAUTS WOULD BE CROWDED TOGETHER, EATING, SLEEPING, AND FLOATING AROUND INSIDE A TINY CAPSULE"

If the crew was hungry, cooked portions of beef hash, toast, biscuits, and bacon were freeze-dried in small bags. A device called a fuel cell combined hydrogen and oxygen to make drinking water. This was injected into the bag and then the contents were squeezed into the mouth.

When he wanted to sleep, each astronaut climbed into a sleeping bag. These had to be strapped to the wall of the capsule to stop them floating around in the weightlessness of space. Going to the bathroom involved an awkward array of plastic bags and hosepipes, something most of the astronauts have chosen not to talk about after returning to Earth.

"IT DIDN'T NEED TO BE STREAMLINED OR AERODYNAMIC BECAUSE THERE IS NO AIR IN SPACE"

Four days into the flight, Armstrong and Aldrin struggled into their space suits and went through a hatch into the last piece of the rocket. Code-named Eagle, this was the lunar module, a strange, angular spacecraft designed to fly down to the moon's surface. Weird-looking, with spindly metal legs and flat feet, it didn't need to be streamlined or aerodynamic because there is no air in space.

Collins remained in the capsule, orbiting the moon on his own. As his colleagues traveled the 69 miles down to the surface, they prepared to do something no one in human history had ever done before: step foot on something other than Earth.

THE EAGLE HAS LANDED

"ONE SMALL STEP FOR MAN, ONE GIANT LEAP FOR MANKIND"

Nearing the surface, Armstrong realized the landing site was covered with boulders. Some of the rocks were as large as cars and might have damaged the Eagle, so the former navy test pilot spent the last few moments skillfully flying it to a safer spot.

"SOME OF THE ROCKS WERE AS LARGE AS BOULDERS AND MIGHT HAVE DAMAGED THE EAGLE"

The two men had been ordered to take a rest in their hammocks before going outside. By standing on the surface, they would be putting themselves in a dangerous place. Only their heavy suits stood between them and temperatures, which ranged from well over boiling point in the sun's glare to -280°F in the shade.

Unlike Earth, the moon has no atmosphere and therefore no oxygen to breathe, so each space suit had a life-support system with a special backpack containing oxygen. Their "fishbowl" helmets gave them a good view of the moon's landscape, and each of their helmet visors contained a thin layer of gold to protect the men's eyes from the blinding sunlight. Inside each helmet, there was even a small piece of rough material that could be used to scratch an itchy nose when it was impossible to use their fingers.

"TEMPERATURES RANGED FROM WELL OVER BOILING POINT IN THE SUN'S GLARE TO −280°F IN THE SHADE"

Eleven layers of different fabrics protected the astronauts from everything from moondust to spacecraft fire to small pieces of flying rock called micrometeroids. But this meant each suit weighed 180 pounds, nearly as much as the astronauts themselves! Even in low gravity, the heavy suits would make it really difficult to move around.

Their space suits offered some protection, but the men still had to have their wits about them in such dangerous conditions. The astronauts rested for four hours after the lunar module had landed. Then Armstrong left the safety of the Eagle to become the first person ever to walk on the moon.

Jumping down to the powdery surface, he sent back a famous message, calling it "one small step for man, one giant leap for mankind." When Aldrin followed him nearly twenty minutes later, the two men joked about not locking themselves out of their spacecraft by mistake.

In spite of their heavy suits, the experience of being on the moon was amazing. Aldrin described the view as "magnificent desolation"—an endless rock-strewn desert beneath a black, airless sky—and Armstrong said that looking back at our tiny planet, "I didn't feel like a giant, I felt very, very small."

"ALDRIN DESCRIBED THE VIEW AS 'MAGNIFICENT DESOLATION'"

Neither man knew it yet, but hundreds of thousands of miles away, more than half a billion people were watching flickering black-and-white television images of them walking around.

Many of those watching must have thought this would never happen. It was only sixty-six years since the first ever airplane was flown by Wilbur Wright—it had flown just a few yards and the flight lasted only twelve seconds—and now these men had made it all the way to the moon. Two tiny pieces of Wright's plane traveled with the astronauts to mark this amazing achievement.

However, after such an incredible journey, they were given less than three hours to explore before it was time for the Eagle to lift off the surface and rejoin Collins orbiting high above.

Because of the problems they'd had landing, there was barely enough fuel left to take off again when it was time to return to the spacecraft. Also, somehow one of Eagle's launch controls had snapped off, but Aldrin jammed an ordinary pen into the socket and luckily this worked. Collins watched nervously as what he called the little golden bug came closer and closer. Soon, after the two spacecraft joined back together, he was able to welcome them back into the capsule.

It took the three astronauts another three days to make the return journey. The lunar module and the service module—the long cylinder beneath the cone-shaped command module—were abandoned out in space. The only part of the huge Saturn V rocket left was the command module, which reentered the Earth's atmosphere at a speed of more than 24,000 miles per hour, and splashed down safely in the Pacific Ocean.

THIS SPECTACULAR, UNREAL WORLD

"YOU'RE JUST FLOATING THERE IN TOTAL DARKNESS... AND IT'S MARVELOUS."

By the time Apollo 11's capsule splashed down, eight days after launch, three more astronauts were already preparing for a second moon landing.

Charles Conrad, Alan Bean, and Dick Gordon traveled on board Apollo 12, which took off four months later. The launch occurred during a storm and two powerful bolts of lightning struck the rocket within seconds of liftoff. Terrifying alarms sounded on board and dozens of warning lights lit up the capsule, but incredibly, the damage wasn't serious and the three crew members were soon on their way.

Their landing on the moon, however, went according to plan and was perfect. Lunar module Intrepid was right on target, placing Conrad and Bean a short walk away from an unmanned probe called Surveyor 3, which had been sent to the moon two years previously.

Alone in the capsule, Gordon joked that he was "glad to be rid of them for 42 hours" but later admitted he was disappointed that he couldn't go down with them. Having flown all that way, he says, "I still had 60 miles to go."

"'I STILL HAD 60 MILES TO GO'"

But his own experience was still amazing. Only six people have ever orbited the moon on their own. For nearly an hour, as a spacecraft travels around the far side of the moon, all communication with Earth is lost.

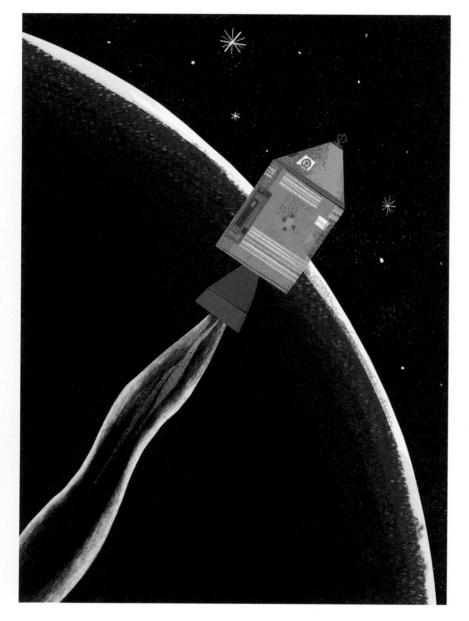

"IT COULD GET LONELY, BUT AS GORDON DISCOVERED, IT WAS ALSO WONDERFUL, SITTING ALONE IN THE DARKNESS 'WITH THE WHOLE UNIVERSE OUTSIDE YOUR WINDOW'"

At this point, the silence and the isolation are total. It could get lonely, but as Gordon discovered, it was also wonderful, sitting alone in the darkness "with the whole universe outside your window."

Down on the surface, his colleagues were scheduled to get more than twice as much time on the moon as Apollo 11's crew had been allowed. Determined to enjoy it, Conrad shouted "whoopee" as he left Intrepid for the first time, and joked about Armstrong's small step being a big one for him because he had shorter legs.

Once both men were outside, they appeared to be having such a good time, laughing and joking about their strange, new, weightless world, that Mission Control had to tell them to quiet down.

"EARTH LOOKED LIKE A GLEAMING BLUE—AND—WHITE EYE, SLOWLY OPENING AND CLOSING'"

Moving around in low gravity certainly looked like a lot of fun. The heavy suits made normal walking impossible, and astronauts soon found the best way was to slowly hop from one foot to the other. If one of them tripped, he fell to the ground very slowly and then had to perform a strange bouncing movement in order to get back up again.

Unlike Apollo 11's crew, the Apollo 12 pair had time to enjoy the experience. Bean found it all slightly unreal, like he was dreaming. To him, the Earth looked like a gleaming blue-and-white eye, slowly opening and closing, and he found he was muttering to himself, "This is the moon, I'm really here, I'm really here." Like many of those listening to the astronauts' excited chatter on the radio, he could hardly believe it was true.

But Bean had to work as well, and like Conrad, he had a small notepad attached to his sleeve reminding him what to do. This contained several jokes from friends at Mission Control but was mostly lists of scientific experiments that had to be set up.

Tests carried out on the surface included experiments to study "moonquakes" and to measure the strength of the moon's magnetic field. The astronauts hoped to find out more about any gases that were present in this strange new world. They were also instructed to collect rock samples and moondust to bring back to be studied.

Known as regolith, moondust caused quite a few problems. It was incredibly fine, and whenever it was kicked up by an astronaut's boot, it took a very long time to settle. Because the individual grains were sharp and gritty, they stuck to everything.

Bean and Conrad tried to brush the stuff off before returning to the Intrepid but found they couldn't. The more they tried the more it worked its way into the material of their space suits. Later, when it was time to go back up to the command module, Gordon told them they were too dirty to come into his spacecraft. Before beginning the journey home, both had to strip off and leave their grubby suits behind in the lunar module.

From then on, all future missions took a special brush with them to the moon.

DISASTER

"A LOUD BANG, 200,000 MILES FROM EARTH"

Listening to Conrad and Bean laughing and joking, it is easy to forget how dangerous and difficult space travel can be.

Astronauts all knew this, though, and one of the items left behind on the moon's surface by the Apollo missions is a shiny metal plaque commemorating fourteen American astronauts and Soviet cosmonauts who had died on other missions.

The next launch, Apollo 13, provided another terrifying reminder of the terrible dangers when, on the third day of the mission, one of its oxygen tanks exploded with a loud bang. No one was injured, but the service module was badly damaged and all radio communication was lost with Earth, more than 200,000 miles behind the spacecraft.

"HOUSTON, WE'VE HAD A PROBLEM HERE"

The radio was fixed in under two seconds, but as they sent a famous message—"Houston, we've had a problem here"—it was clear that Jim Lovell, Jack Swigert, and Fred Haise could not continue their journey to the moon.

"IT WAS CLEAR THAT THEY COULD NOT CONTINUE THEIR JOURNEY TO THE MOON"

The disappointment was obvious, but far more frightening was the possibility that the damage caused by the explosion meant they might not be able to fly back home either.

Looking out of the command module capsule's tiny windows, the crew could already see oxygen escaping out into space. They had enough left to breathe but more was needed to power the fuel cells used to make electricity and drinking water, which were crucial for their survival.

"THE CREW'S ONLY HOPE OF SURVIVAL WAS TO USE THE SPACECRAFT'S LAST REMAINING ROCKET BOOSTER TO GET BACK ON COURSE FOR EARTH"

The three men calmly climbed into the lunar module, Aquarius, which they hoped to use as a kind of lifeboat. The idea was to switch off everything in the command module to preserve it for the final stage of their return journey. But to return at all, they first had to find a way to get back into orbit around the Earth.

The crew's only hope of survival was to use the spacecraft's last remaining rocket booster to get back on course for Earth. Nothing like this had ever been attempted before, and it was impossible to know whether or not it would work with such a small engine.

"THE MATHEMATICS TO DO THIS HAD TO BE COMPLETELY ACCURATE, AS THE CREW HAD ONLY ONE CHANCE TO GET IT RIGHT"

Down on the ground, hundreds of NASA staff worked around the clock.

They were trying to calculate precisely how and when the little rocket should be fired to maximize the astronauts' chances of survival. The mathematics had to be completely accurate, as the crew had only one chance to get it right. For four days, no one went home or snatched more than a few minutes' sleep on the floor beneath the desks.

Meanwhile, thousands of miles out in space, the astronauts faced another, more immediate danger. Conditions on board Aquarius were even more uncomfortable than usual. With the main computer switched off to save power, it quickly grew damp inside and extremely cold. More importantly, Aquarius had been designed to accommodate two men for a day and

"THEIR AIR SUPPLY WAS TURNING POISONOUS, AS THE LEVEL OF DEADLY CARBON DIOXIDE ROSE HIGHER AND HIGHER"

a half, not three men for four days. They didn't have enough air filters, and already their air

supply was turning poisonous, as the level of deadly carbon dioxide rose higher and higher.

The command module capsule was fitted with special filters called scrubbers that could have solved the problem, except they were square, and the hoses needed to activate them in the lunar module were round. However, by using socks, plastic bags, and some sticky tape, Mission Control showed the astronauts how to build an adaptor to fit a square peg into a round hole, and keep their air supply safe for a bit longer.

It looked messy, but it was a brilliant solution and one that kept the exhausted crewmen alive in their cold, uncomfortable lifeboat. Eventually Mission Control managed to figure out when to fire the last remaining rocket, and for how long.

Finally, after many tense hours, the decision was taken to fire it, and Apollo 13 slowly began to move closer to Earth. The men returned to the command module capsule from the Aquarius, and after separating from the damaged rocket section, they reentered the

Earth's atmosphere in the normal way. But even now, no one could be sure they were safe because their parachutes might have been damaged in the explosion.

The minutes ticked by until finally the capsule was spotted high above the ocean with all three parachutes open and working. Disaster had been averted, and the three astronauts were pulled alive from the capsule moments after it splashed down in the sea.

Apollo 13 may not have reached the moon, but the crew had survived against almost-impossible odds. Thanks to a combination of ingenuity, calm, and really astonishing courage, they had come home.

SCIENCE *on the* MOON

"SOMEBODY SAID A BILLION YEARS, AND I THOUGHT, HUH? NOTHING'S THAT OLD"

The idea of people walking on the moon was enormously exciting, for television viewers as well as for the astronauts, but slowly the sense of adventure gave way to more serious exploration.

Despite the near disaster of Apollo 13, another mission was planned. Apollo 14 was to be the first landing devoted entirely to science. As the others had before them, Alan Shepard and Edgar Mitchell both wore lists on their sleeves with instructions for the various experiments they had to carry out on the moon's surface. For the first time, a small two-wheeled cart was carried on the lunar module. This was used for transporting rock samples as well as all the tools and cameras they needed.

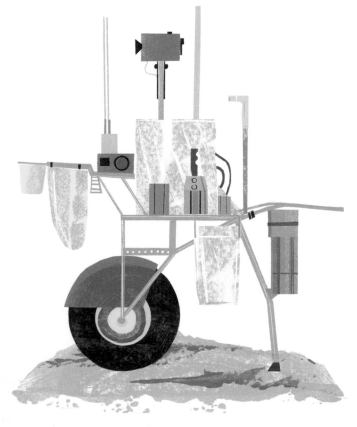

Orbiting miles above them, Stuart Roosa was kept busy taking hundreds of spectacular photographs of the moon, trying to identify possible future landing sites. He also had about 500 seeds with him in the command module. Scientists wanted to know whether being in space would harm a plant's ability to germinate and grow when they were returned to Earth.

"SCIENTISTS WANTED TO KNOW WHETHER BEING IN SPACE WOULD HARM A PLANT'S ABILITY TO GERMINATE AND GROW"

This experiment was a success—nearly all the seeds still grew after being in space, and eventually several hundred special "moon trees" were planted in parks and forests across the U.S. These included some redwoods, the world's tallest tree.

During their two trips out from the lunar module, Shepard and Mitchell pulled their cart about 2 miles.

"EVENTUALLY SEVERAL HUNDRED SPECIAL 'MOON TREES' WERE PLANTED ACROSS THE U.S."

Walking farther than any of the earlier astronauts, they collected some rock fragments that were found to be billions of years old. Flying through space and crashing down onto the moon long before people or even dinosaurs existed on Earth, giant rocks like these had formed many of the gigantic craters that we can still see on the surface.

Even with the cart, collecting rock and soil samples for study back on Earth was exhausting work, especially as they collected an enormous 94 pounds of it.

However, the astronauts found time to play around a bit as well. Shepard had somehow managed to smuggle a golf club onto the spacecraft, which he used to hit a couple of balls. This was the first time anyone had ever played a sport on the moon. Swinging the club properly was tricky in a space suit, but in the low gravity and with no air to slow them down, it seemed to Shepard as if the balls flew for miles and miles.

Watching film of the mission, which for the first time was seen in color, it is also clear that both men found it a deeply moving experience being alone in this silent, magical world. When it was over, and he and his companions had returned safely, Shepard admitted that standing on the moon and looking up at Earth for the first time he had actually cried.

"HE WAS STUNNED BY HOW BEAUTIFUL THE EARTH LOOKED FROM SO FAR AWAY"

Such a strong emotion took him completely by surprise, but Mitchell experienced something similar. In particular, he was stunned by how beautiful the Earth looked from so far away, a sparkling sky-blue, emerald-green, and white jewel moving slowly through an ocean of soft, velvety black.

As Apollo's Jim Lovell had noticed, from this distance, the Earth looked so small that "Everything that you've ever known, your loved ones, your business, the problems of the Earth itself," he said, all this could disappear behind a person's thumb.

"BUT HE WAS LEFT WITH A POWERFUL FEELING THAT IN SOME MYSTERIOUS WAY THE MOON HAD BEEN WAITING SILENTLY"

As the pair began to prepare for their return journey, Mitchell felt a sudden sadness, something he called "a strange nostalgia" for this ancient, alien world. He knew how dangerous it was out there, they both did after spending their few precious hours amid the airless, lifeless craters. But he was left with a powerful feeling that in some mysterious way the moon had been waiting silently for millions of years just to welcome its first few human visitors.

Returning to the command module, the two men realized they both felt slightly miserable. Each knew he was leaving somewhere very special and would never return.

DRIVING *on the* MOON

"EVERY TIME WE HIT A ROCK WE WOULD SAIL THROUGH SPACE."

No one stayed on the moon for very long. An Apollo mission lasted for up to twelve days, but most of that time was spent flying to the moon and back again. Only two or three days were spent on the moon's surface, where bulky space suits made moving around exhausting. This meant none of the astronauts was able to walk very far before having to return to the base.

To solve this problem, David Scott, Jim Irwin, and Alfred Worden were given a small battery-powered vehicle. It was called a lunar rover, but nicknamed "moon buggy." It was folded up and attached to the lunar module Falcon, and looked a bit like a go-kart with deckchair seats and chunky tires made of metal mesh instead of rubber. There was room on board for two men with their cameras and scientific equipment, and also for the heavy bags of soil and moon rock that they started to collect as they drove around the surface.

The moon buggy was one of the slowest vehicles ever built, with a top speed of only 8 miles per hour. But it still sounds like a moon buggy must have been a lot of fun to drive. Low gravity means that even a small bump could be quite exciting.

Returning to Earth after trying it out, Irwin described how "every time we hit a rock or a bump we would sail through space." On several occasions, the buggy nearly flipped right over.

The moon buggies might have been some of the slowest cars ever built in the solar system, but they were also the most expensive, costing $38 million each. One of the reasons they cost so much to build is that everything carried on a rocket is designed to be as light as possible, because the lighter the rocket, the easier it is to escape Earth's gravity at launch. This meant using unusual metal alloys instead of steel like a normal car, and a tiny electric motor mounted inside each wheel. Another two motors steered the buggy, which the driver controlled by using a joystick mounted between the seats. The astronauts complained their space suits made it hard to put on the seat belts. Instead of maps, they used photographs of the moon to find their way around.

"INSTEAD OF MAPS, THEY USED PHOTOGRAPHS OF THE MOON TO FIND THEIR WAY AROUND"

During the mission, David Scott and Jim Irwin went out in the buggy three times, covering just over 17 miles. It doesn't sound like much, not for all that money, and the two men were told not to go too far because if it broke down they would have to walk back to the Falcon. However, being able to drive meant the men could explore a much wider area than had been possible on previous missions. Their discoveries included the incredible "Genesis rock," which was more than four billion years old.

"WITHOUT ANY AIR TO SLOW AN OBJECT DOWN, EVERYTHING FALLS AT THE SAME SPEED"

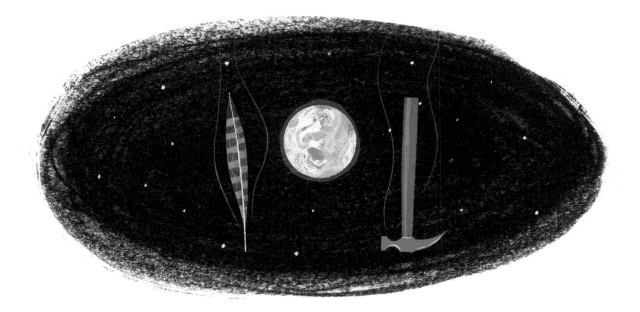

On their final outing, Scott also carried out a fascinating experiment by dropping a falcon's feather and a hammer to see which hit the ground first. Strangely they landed at exactly the same moment because on the moon, without any air to slow an object down, everything falls at the same speed.

After this, the buggy was parked for the last time, about 300 feet from the Falcon. From there, its camera filmed the lunar module taking off before beaming the pictures back to Earth. Even though the moon buggies were so expensive to make, they were left behind and are still parked on the moon. There is one each from Apollo 15, Apollo 16, and Apollo 17. A fourth was never used and is displayed in a Washington, D.C., museum.

BLINDING, BEAUTIFUL BLACK

"I'VE NEVER SEEN A DAY THAT'S AS CLEAR AS A DAY ON THE MOON"

By the time Apollo 16 was ready to take off, people were becoming used to the idea of men walking on the moon. It no longer seemed quite so extraordinary for a rocket to fly at 24,000 miles per hour to reach such an amazing place.

But to the astronauts, there was nothing at all ordinary about their mission. While Ken Mattingly spent more than five days in the command module, orbiting the moon a record sixty-four times, John Young and Charlie Duke were able to spend the longest time yet down on the surface, exploring what is called the Descartes region—a hilly area in the southeast of the moon.

> "KEN MATTINGLY SPENT MORE THAN FIVE DAYS IN THE COMMAND MODULE, ORBITING THE MOON A RECORD 64 TIMES"

Duke's excitement was obvious the moment he climbed down from the lunar module Orion. "Fantastic," he radioed back to Earth, "oh, that first foot on the lunar surface is super!" He and Young quickly began to unpack their moon buggy for its first excursion. This was scheduled to last more than seven hours, nearly three times as long as the total time Apollo 11's crew had been allowed to spend outside.

> "'OH, THAT FIRST FOOT ON THE LUNAR SURFACE IS SUPER!'"

There were several experiments to carry out on the surface, but one failed when an astronaut tripped over a cable and broke it. (Space suits made it very difficult for the men to see their feet when they were walking around.) The most enjoyable experiment involved the moon buggy, which Young had permission to drive farther and faster than ever before.

This "Grand Prix" test involved doing skids and tight turns as well as braking hard to see how the vehicle performed. The driving itself went well, but when Young finished, he was covered in moondust because one of the wheel covers had been slightly damaged.

Several other experiments were carried out too, which seem less fun but were just as important. Special equipment was used to establish the composition of the moon's surface and its atmosphere, and to measure tiny differences in the moon's gravity in various different places.

As excursion times grew longer, it was easy for astronauts to become confused and disorientated. Without any weather or air pollution, they could see for miles across the surface, but it was impossible to judge distances accurately. A nearby hill looked the same as a distant mountain, and the black sky (and even blacker shadows) made it hard to navigate in this weird, unfamiliar landscape.

Before leaving Earth, Duke had had a very strange dream. In it, he and Young were driving the buggy around when they discovered some tire tracks in the dust, which they decided to follow. Before long, they came to another buggy and found themselves face-to-face with two other astronauts. Duke thought they looked just like him and Young, but it was as if they had been sitting there, waiting, for thousands of years.

"THE MOST SPECTACULARLY BEAUTIFUL DESERT YOU COULD EVER IMAGINE"

It sounds a bit spooky, but once he was on the moon, Duke loved everything about what he called "the most spectacularly beautiful desert you could ever imagine." He found the rocks glittered in the unfiltered sunshine, and he felt so at home there he had to resist the urge to take off his helmet, which would have killed him very quickly. Without a helmet, an astronaut wouldn't be able to breathe, but also the conditions on the moon would cause his blood to boil along with any other liquid such as the spit on his tongue or the sweat on his skin.

The funny thing about Duke's dream is that if the tire marks he imagined he saw had been genuine they really would last for thousands or even millions of years. With no wind, there is nothing at all to disturb the surface and so nothing moves on the moon except the shadows.

"SO NOTHING MOVES ON THE MOON EXCEPT THE SHADOWS"

This means that everything the astronauts left behind is still there today—even their individual footprints.

Duke realized this and decided to put a photograph of his family down on the ground near the landing site. On the back of it, he wrote a message in the hope that one day it will be found by someone else visiting the moon in the future. *This is the family of Astronaut Duke from Planet Earth*, the message reads. *Landed on the moon, April 1972.*

Unfortunately, the photograph is not the only thing the two men left there. Before stepping out of the Orion at the start of their first moonwalk, Duke had handed Young something called a jettison bag. This was full of Apollo 16's trash, and like similar bags from previous missions this too will still be lying there on the ground in thousands and thousands of years' time.

LAST MEN *on the* MOON

"LET'S ENJOY IT. LET'S NOT WORRY ABOUT GOING HOME UNTIL GOING-HOME TIME COMES."

When people heard that Apollo 17 was going to be the final mission to the moon, a crowd of half a million turned up to see the launch. For the first time, this took place after dark, and as the rocket lit up the night sky, a red streak could be seen from over 500 miles away.

It was also unusual because some small furry passengers joined crew members Gene Cernan, Ronald Evans, and Harrison Schmitt in the capsule. Five mice, Fe, Fi, Fo, Fum, and Phooey, were part of an experiment looking at the effects of space travel.

The mission was scheduled to be the longest so far, at just over twelve and a half days. During this time, Cernan and Harrison would get to spend more than three days on the surface, becoming the last men to walk on the moon.

Before Apollo 17, the astronauts had all been military pilots, but Schmitt was a scientist. His speciality was geology, and his wife suggested he apply for the job, as his training would be useful when examining rock samples from each of the missions.

"DURING THE JOURNEY, HE TOOK ONE OF THE MOST FAMOUS PHOTOGRAPHS OF ALL TIME"

Schmitt was chosen from hundreds of other scientists to become the first one to fly to the moon. During the journey, he took one of the most famous photographs of all time. It's called *The Blue Marble* and shows Earth from 28,000 miles away. Since then, people all over the world have been able to see this breathtaking image of the oceans and continents seen through swirling white clouds.

"SINCE THEN, PEOPLE ALL OVER THE WORLD HAVE BEEN ABLE TO SEE THIS BREATHTAKING IMAGE OF THE OCEANS AND CONTINENTS SEEN THROUGH SWIRLING WHITE CLOUDS"

He and Cernan were determined to enjoy themselves once they got to the moon. After leaving the lunar module Challenger, they could be heard singing a song called "The Fountain in the Park." This starts with the line "While strolling in the park one day," but Schmitt changed this to "I was strolling on the moon one day." Cernan joined in until the pair forgot the rest of the words and got on with their work.

The site chosen for Apollo 17 was called Taurus-Littrow, and it was picked because it was thought that rocks both older and younger than those previously returned from other Apollo missions might be found there. This time the scientific experiments included setting off several small explosions to find out more about the rocky surface. The moon usually looks white or gray to us, but some of the rock samples collected during earlier missions contained strange green, black, and even maroon material. Now, during one of the excursions in the moon buggy, Schmitt found something even more remarkable—soil that was actually orange.

"SCHMITT FOUND SOMETHING EVEN MORE REMARKABLE—SOIL THAT WAS ACTUALLY ORANGE"

At first he thought he was imagining the color (sunlight can play funny tricks with our eyes), but Cernan saw it too. After studying a sample that the men brought back, scientists eventually decided

"THE MOON BUGGY LOOKS LIKE A LITTLE TOY"

the bright orange soil was probably formed by a gigantic volcano erupting on the moon more than three billion years ago. Even now, scientists are discovering surprising things about the rocks that were collected from the moon.

Many photographs were taken on Apollo 17. Along with *The Blue Marble*, one of the most extraordinary shows Schmitt standing next to a boulder the size of a bungalow. He appears tiny in comparison, and the moon buggy looks like a little toy. With the empty lunar desert stretching out behind, and the sweeping black sky above, it is a wonderful but lonely image of the last ever moonwalk.

Sadly, for those whose expertise and determination had made the Apollo adventure such a success, and for the millions of people back on Earth who had watched it unfolding on their screens, this was to be the final mission to the moon. To commemorate this, a plaque was left behind when the astronauts set off for home. Signed by the three men and by President Richard Nixon, it read "Here Man completed his first explorations of the moon, December 1972 AD. May the spirit of peace in which we came be reflected in the lives of all mankind."

"ONE OF THE ASTRONAUTS HAD TO CLIMB OUT OF THE SPACECRAFT WHILE IT WAS TRAVELING BACK FROM THE MOON"

While all this was going on, Evans was orbiting the moon and waiting for his colleagues to return. He was also preparing for an amazing experience of his own, a spacewalk more than 200,000 miles from home. Special cameras were fitted to the outside of the command and service modules, and the film in these needed to be brought into the capsule before it reentered Earth's atmosphere. To do this, one of the astronauts had to climb out of the spacecraft while it was traveling back from the moon.

Being on the outside of a spacecraft hurtling at over a thousand miles per hour might sound terrifying to us, but the lack of air in space meant that Evans had no sense at all of the speed the spacecraft was hurtling back to Earth. Without any air resistance, it felt as if the spacecraft wasn't moving at all.

But for more than an hour, attached to the spacecraft by only a thin tether supplying oxygen and power, he must have had an incredible view of the universe. The moon behind him, the sky full of stars, and the Earth growing larger and larger as the last Apollo mission neared its end.

Chapter 10

A PRECIOUS LEGACY

"EVERY GUY THAT HAS GONE OUT TO LUNAR DISTANCE IS AMAZED BY THE BEAUTY OF THE EARTH"

The safe return of Apollo 17 marked the end of the great adventure. In the fifty years since, no one else has walked on the moon. No one else has seen our planet from so far away or been able to marvel at its fragile beauty.

"EVERYWHERE THEY WENT THE ASTRONAUTS WERE TOLD, 'WE DID IT.' NOT YOU DID IT, OR AMERICA DID IT—BUT WE DID IT."

The twelve who were lucky enough to experience this, whose bravery and skill enabled them to make this giant leap into the unknown, were greeted as heroes when they returned. Everywhere they went people lined up to see them and to hear them speak. Everywhere they went the astronauts were told, "We did it." Not you did it, or America did it—but we did it.

People said it this way because for those who had watched the dramatic television pictures of the moonwalks, or been close enough to see the gigantic Saturn V rockets blasting off, the amazing Apollo adventure seemed like something people all around the world could share.

"THEIR SUCCESS DEMONSTRATED PEOPLE'S DESIRE TO DISCOVER MORE ABOUT THE UNIVERSE AND OUR DETERMINATION TO EXPLORE"

Standing on the moon was not simply an achievement for one country or for twelve men but an important achievement for all mankind. The U.S. may have begun by wanting to show the Soviet Union and the rest of the world how smart its scientists and pilots were, but in the end, their success demonstrated people's desire to discover more about the universe and our determination to explore.

The bravery of the astronauts was truly astonishing, but so was the hard work and incredible ingenuity of the hundreds of thousands of mathematicians, scientists, and engineers who made the lunar landings possible. Getting to the moon and back was something everyone could celebrate: it had taken more than a million years of evolution, a million years of gazing up at the night sky, but humans had finally walked on a world other than our own.

The expense of doing it was enormous. In fact it has been estimated that each minute spent on the surface cost the equivalent of $22 million. That's more than $367,000 per second.

This is one of the reasons why no one has ever been back to bounce around among the craters. There have been other launches and other missions, and today's International Space Station—an incredible orbiting laboratory—is certainly an extraordinary creation. But even this is a thousand times nearer than the moon. Smaller rockets fly up to it every few weeks, and hundreds of people from nearly twenty different countries have so far made the journey.

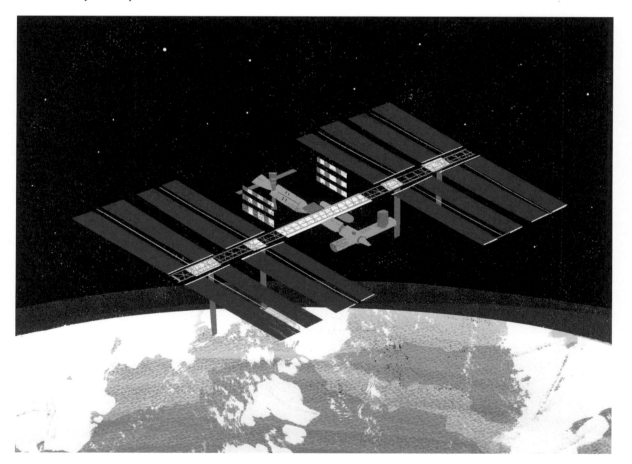

Spending time living on the space station must be exciting, but it is nothing like flying to the moon—which is still more difficult, more expensive, and far more dangerous than most people can imagine. By proving it could be done, the Apollo astronauts thrilled television audiences around the world, but more importantly, their example paved the way for future missions to take men and women farther and farther out into space.

Exactly where these may take us is still unclear. China is now planning its own moon landing, and Orion, a new, even more powerful spacecraft, could eventually take its American crew of four even farther afield.

The most exciting developments, however, are focused on Mars. Building on their experiences of Saturn V and Apollo, teams of engineers in the U.S. are already working on the technologies needed to enable humans to fly to the famous "red planet" and to live and work on its surface before returning home.

As with the lunar landings the challenges are enormous: Mars is more than 35 million miles away, meaning it can take nearly a year just to get there. But if Apollo showed us anything, it is that with a combination of courage, determination, and ingenuity we can and will go far.

APOLLO 11

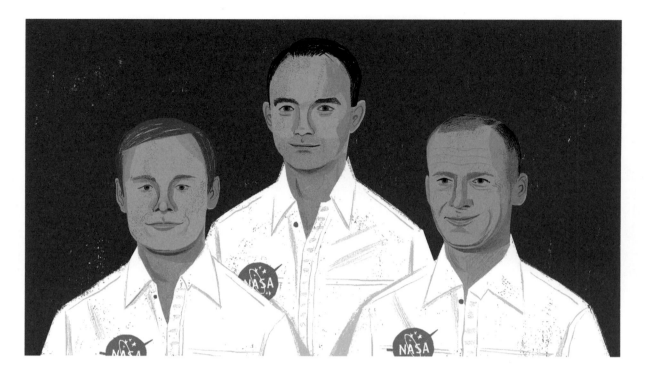

NEIL ARMSTRONG (COMMANDER)

The first human to step on the moon, Neil Armstrong was born in Wapakoneta, Ohio, in 1930. He took his first airplane ride at age six and became a skilled pilot, flying over 200 different models of aircraft including jets, rockets, helicopters, and gliders. He performed the first successful docking of two vehicles in space before the Apollo 11 mission. He passed away in 2012, at age eighty-two.

MICHAEL COLLINS (COMMAND MODULE PILOT)

Born in Rome, Italy, in 1930 Michael Collins joined the U.S. Air Force before he became an astronaut in 1963. His first trip into space was on a two-man capsule and included two moonwalks. On Apollo 11, Collins remained aboard the command module while Armstrong and Aldrin walked on the moon. He left NASA in 1970 and was the director of the National Air & Space Museum, Smithsonian Institution, in Washington, D.C., for seven years.

EDWIN "BUZZ" ALDRIN (LUNAR MODULE PILOT)

Buzz Aldrin served in the Korean War and got a Ph.D. from the Massachusetts Institute of Technology (MIT) before being chosen as an astronaut. On the Apollo 11 mission, he flew the lunar module down to the moon and was the second person to walk on its surface. He retired from NASA in 1971 and has since written a number of books including two autobiographies and a history of the Apollo program.

APOLLO 12

CHARLES PETE CONRAD (COMMANDER)

Conrad suffered with dyslexia when he was a child and was expelled from one school after failing most of his eleventh-grade exams. However, he earned his pilot's certificate before even graduating and became a world-famous astronaut, aeronautical engineer, naval officer, and businessman. He set an eight-day space endurance record on his first spaceflight and became the third person to walk on the moon. He died in 1999.

ALAN BEAN (LUNAR MODULE PILOT)

A test pilot in the U.S. Navy, Alan Bean was one of fourteen trainees selected by NASA for its third group of astronauts in October 1963. He was the fourth person to walk on the moon and went back into space again for the second crewed flight to the United States' first space station, Skylab. After retiring from NASA, he created famous Apollo-themed paintings including boot prints and small pieces of moondust. He died in 2018.

DICK GORDON (COMMAND MODULE PILOT)

Remembered as one of the the nation's "boldest flyers," Gordon was so relaxed in space that he even fell asleep during a break in his second spacewalk! After retiring from NASA, he became executive vice president of the New Orleans Saints football team and worked in oil, gas, engineering, and technology companies. He died in 2017.

APOLLO 13

JIM LOVELL (COMMANDER)

Jim Lovell was actually scheduled to command Apollo 14, but the crews were swapped as it was felt that the commander of the other crew, Alan Shepard, needed more time to train after experiencing an ear problem. As the commander of Apollo 8, Lovell is one of only three people to have flown to the moon twice, and because of the ill-fated Apollo 13 mission, the only one to have flown there twice without making a landing.

FRED HAISE (LUNAR MODULE PILOT)

Fred Haise originally planned to be a journalist but became a naval aviation cadet in 1952 and served as a fighter pilot. During his life, Haise has spent a whopping 9,300 hours flying. Because of the distance the three astronauts on Apollo 13 traveled around the moon in their attempt to get back to Earth, they likely hold the record for the farthest distance from Earth ever traveled by human beings.

JACK SWIGERT (COMMAND MODULE PILOT)

Famously, Jack Swigert was called on to replace Ken Mattingly as the command module pilot at the last minute after Mattingly was exposed to German measles. Before becoming an astronaut in 1966, Swigert was a U.S. Air Force pilot in Japan and Korea. He retired from NASA in 1977 and was later elected to the House of Representatives, shortly before his death from cancer in 1982.

APOLLO 14

ALAN SHEPARD (COMMANDER)

Age 47 at the time of Apollo 14, Alan Shepard was the oldest astronaut to have flown in space and had to overcome a rare condition of the inner ear called Ménière's disease before he was allowed on the mission. However, no one could doubt his experience. He was one of the original seven astronauts recruited by NASA in the late 1950s, known as the Mercury Seven, and was the first American in space in 1961. He died in 1998 of leukemia.

EDGAR MITCHELL (LUNAR MODULE PILOT)

Mitchell joined the space program after serving in the U.S. Navy. During the Apollo 14 mission, Mitchell was part of a team that set records for the most time (33 hours) and longest distance traveled on the lunar surface. He retired from the space program in 1972, and went on to devote his time to his interest in the paranormal, even setting up a research institute to do this in 1977. He died in 2016.

STUART ROOSA (COMMAND MODULE PILOT)

Neither Stuart Roosa nor lunar module pilot Mitchell had any space flight experience when they were chosen by Shepard to be part of his crew for Apollo 14. Roosa worked as a firefighter for the U.S. forest service and a captain in the U.S. Air Force before being accepted for NASA's fifth group of astronauts in 1966. After retiring as an astronaut, he moved to Greece to work in business. He died in 1994, at age sixty-one.

APOLLO 15

DAVID SCOTT (COMMANDER)

David Scott was born in Texas in 1932. He served in the U.S. Air Force and was one of the third group of astronauts selected by NASA in October 1963. He flew in space with Neil Armstrong on the Gemini 8 mission and was command module pilot for Apollo 9 before becoming the seventh person to walk on the moon on Apollo 15.

ALFRED WORDEN (COMMAND MODULE PILOT)

Alfred Worden worked in the air force before he was chosen for the Apollo 15 mission. He orbited the moon seventy-five times, which took him 2,235 miles away from the surface and set a record (at the time) for being the farthest away from any other human beings.

JIM IRWIN (LUNAR MODULE PILOT)

When he was a little boy, in Pittsburgh, Pennsylvania, Jim Irwin remembers being laughed at for wanting to go to the moon. However, he ended up being the eighth person to walk on it. Struck by the Earth's beauty, he was deeply affected by his time on the moon, and he resigned from NASA in July 1972 to form a religious organization. He died in 1991 of a heart attack.

APOLLO 16

JOHN YOUNG (COMMANDER)

John Young was the first person to fly into space six times and spent more than 800 hours away from Earth. He commanded the first space shuttle mission in 1981 and the first Spacelab mission in 1983 and remained an active astronaut until the late 1980s, eventually retiring from NASA in 2004. He died in 2018.

THOMAS K. MATTINGLY (COMMAND MODULE PILOT)

Born in Chicago, Illinois, Ken Mattingly was a student at the Air Force Aerospace Research Pilot School before he became an astronaut. He was originally meant to go on Apollo 13, but exposure to German measles kept him on Earth. His time spent training came in use as he was called upon to find a way of rescuing the crew when their oxygen tank exploded. Apollo 16 gave him his long-awaited chance to fly into space.

CHARLES DUKE (LUNAR MODULE PILOT)

Former test pilot Charles Duke was part of the support team for Apollo 10 and Apollo 11. Age thirty-six during the Apollo 16 mission, he was the youngest person ever to walk on the moon. He left a family photo of his wife and two children on the surface. Since retiring from NASA, he has worked in business and prison ministry.

APOLLO 17

GENE CERNAN (COMMANDER)

The last person ever to walk on the moon, Gene Cernan was also one of only three astronauts to travel there on two occasions, as he successfully orbited it during the Apollo 10 mission. His many awards include the NASA Distinguished Service Medal, induction into the U.S. Space Hall of Fame, and the Wright Brothers Memorial Trophy. He died in 2017.

RONALD EVANS (COMMAND MODULE PILOT)

Ronald Evans, born in St. Francis, Kansas, in 1933, was considered one of the best pilots in the astronaut corps, having flown in over 100 combat missions during the Vietnam War. He holds the record of having done the most time in lunar orbit—he spent over six days orbiting the moon in the command module while Cernan and Schmitt were on the surface. He died in 1990.

HARRISON SCHMITT (LUNAR MODULE PILOT)

Harrison Schmitt differed from the other astronauts as he was a geologist, rather than a test pilot or member of the military. His knowledge helped NASA recognize features of the moon's surface and navigate accordingly. Since walking on the moon, Schmitt has served as senator for New Mexico and is now a college engineering professor.

GLOSSARY

Aerodynamic
Something that has been designed to encounter the least air resistance and therefore go faster.

Atmosphere
A layer of gases that surrounds a planet or moon.

Evolution
The theory that all kinds of living things developed from earlier types, with changes occuring over millions of years.

G-force
This is used to describe the acceleration of something relative to the Earth's gravity. For example, when a plane makes a fast turn, the fast movement can create more than 6G of force, or six times the normal force of Earth's gravity.

Germinate
When seeds begin to sprout and grow.

Gravity
The force that pulls two things toward each other. The more massive an object is, the greater its gravity, which is why the Earth's gravity pulls us to the ground.

Magnetic field
The invisible area affected by a magnet.

Moonquake
The equivalent of an earthquake, but on the moon. Moonquakes are weaker than earthquakes but can last much longer—up to several hours!

Orbit
The movement of an object around another, for example of the moon around Earth or a spacecraft around the moon.

Soviet Union
A powerful country that existed from 1922 to 1991 that included Russia and 14 other republics.

TIMELINE

APRIL 1961

Man in space

Yuri Gagarin becomes the first man
to enter space in Vostok 1

JUNE 1963

Woman in space

Valentina Tereshkova becomes
the first woman in space

MAY 1964

Saturn 1 launch

First flight of an early model of the
Apollo spacecraft (unmanned)

MAY 1971

**First space probe to
land on Mars**

APRIL 1971

Salyut 1

First space station of any kind
launched by the Soviet Union

JANUARY 1971

Apollo 14

Proven that seeds can still
germinate after being in
space

JULY 1971

Apollo 15

First moon
buggies used

APRIL 1972

Apollo 16

Descartes region explored

JANUARY 1968
Apollo 5
First test flight of the
lunar module (unmanned)

OCTOBER 1968
Apollo 7
First crewed flight of the
Apollo spacecraft

JULY 1969
Apollo 11
Humans walk on the moon for
the first time

APRIL 1970
Apollo 13
Mission aborted after oxygen
tank explosions

November 1969
Apollo 12
Lunar exploration
carried out

DECEMBER 1972
Apollo 17
Last mission to the moon

1998–2011
**International Space
Station built**
Largest man-made structure
built in space to date

2012
Interstellar space
Voyager 1 becomes the first
spacecraft to leave our solar
system and enter the space
between stars

Brimming with creative inspiration, how-to projects, and useful information to enrich your everyday life, Quarto Knows is a favorite destination for those pursuing their interests and passions. Visit our site and dig deeper with our books into your area of interest: Quarto Creates, Quarto Cooks, Quarto Homes, Quarto Lives, Quarto Drives, Quarto Explores, Quarto Gifts, or Quarto Kids.

Inspiring | Educating | Creating | Entertaining

First published in 2019 by Wide Eyed Editions, an imprint of The Quarto Group. 400 First Avenue North, Suite 400, Minneapolis, MN 55401, USA. T (612) 344-8100 F (612) 344-8692 **www.QuartoKnows.com**

A catalog record for this book is available from the British Library.

ISBN 978-1-78603-092-4

The illustrations were created digitally

Set in Apercu

Published by Rachel Williams and Jenny Broom
Designed by Nicola Price
Edited by Katie Cotton
Production by Kate O'Riordan and Jenny Cundill

Manufactured in Guangdong, China TT022019

9 8 7 6 5 4 3 2 1